Australian reefs

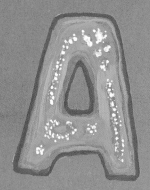

Along the coastline of Australia, underwater reefs—barrier reefs, fringe reefs, atolls, and patch reefs—are bustling with sea life. These rich ecosystems are wonders of nature!

Australian reefs are teeming with sea animals found nowhere else in the world. But many are vulnerable, threatened, or endangered, and their future is at risk.

Ningaloo Reef

Fringing reefs form in shallow waters, usually close to shore.

Patch reefs are small reefs that form in the open ocean.

Reef-building corals are found in warm, shallow water. Deep-sea corals live in cold, dark water and grow slowly.

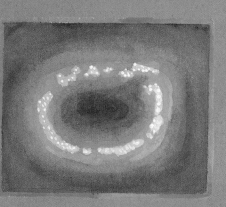

Atolls are rings of coral with open water in the middle.

Montgomery
Reef

Great Barrier Reef

Barrier reefs protect the coastline from large waves. They run parallel to the shore and are separated from it by deep, wide lagoons.

With the help of an underwater robot, scientists have discovered a giant reef, more than 1,640 feet/ 500 meters tall, in the deep waters off the Great Barrier Reef. That's taller than the Empire State Building.

Millions of years ago, many parts of Australia's mainland were underwater. These shallow seas were full of creatures, including giant megalodon sharks and plesiosaurs. Today, fossils of the prehistoric animals that lived and swam along ancient inland reefs are being found.

Great
Southern
Reef

Biodiversity

A reef has the highest biodiversity of any ecosystem on Earth. More than 25 percent of all sea creatures call a coral reef home.

Biodiversity refers to a wide variety of plants and animals that live together and depend on one another to survive. On the reef, each creature has a special job to do. If there are too many, or not enough, of one particular creature, the delicate balance of the reef's biodiversity suffers.

Protecting the biodiversity of life in the sea is a major challenge facing people today.

The biodiversity of Australian reefs is crucial for the survival of sea creatures and the health of the oceans, and it helps people too. Reefs are a source of food and support the fishing industry. They are known as "medicine cabinets" as they are full of cures for treating countless diseases.

Climate change and pollution are the biggest threats to the biodiversity of Australian reefs. Since 2016, half of the shallow corals on the Great Barrier Reef have died at an alarming rate from coral bleaching. This occurs when a rise in ocean temperature stresses the coral. Continued stress may cause the coral polyps to die, leaving many sea creatures homeless.

Coral reefs

Coral reefs are underwater homes to millions of creatures. They are sometimes called the "rain forests of the sea."

The corals that make up a reef might look like plants, but they are actually a living colony of tiny sea animals called coral polyps.

Coral reefs can act as fish nurseries, giving baby fish a safe place to feed and hide until they are big enough to swim out into the wider ocean.

Most coral polyps feed at night. They stretch out their tentacles in search of tiny zooplankton to eat.

There are two kinds of coral animals that
live on a reef: hard corals and soft corals.

Hard corals are the reef builders. Their
bony skeletons look like boulders, pillars,
cacti, antlers, or even giant brains.

Soft corals are the reef decorators. These
brilliantly colored corals look like fans, fingers,
flowers, feathers, or bits of dainty lace.

Dolphins

Dolphins are playful and intelligent marine mammals. Bottlenose dolphins are found in the waters of many Australian reefs.

The sheltered waters of a reef are the perfect place for bottlenose dolphins to find food and care for their calves.

Dolphins use clicks and whistles to communicate with one another. Some dolphins have their own unique whistle and can recognize another dolphin's sound over long distances.

A bottlenose dolphin has a bottle-shaped snout and a smiley curved mouth.

Dolphins are mammals and need oxygen to survive. They can hold their breath for eight to ten minutes underwater before they need to surface for air.

Dolphins are protected in all Australian waters; it is illegal to hurt or interfere with these beloved mammals.

Bottlenose dolphins sometimes create bubble rings with their blowhole. They twirl the rings with their snout, swim through them, and even bite them to make them pop!

Dolphins use echolocation, meaning that they make clicking sounds, and when the sounds hit an object and bounce back to them as an echo, they can use the information they gain to tell the location and size of objects in their environment.

Eels

Eels are snake-like fish that can be found on coral reefs. Most have sharp teeth, strong jaws, and a long, lean body.

Moray eels can be seen poking their head out of a reef, opening and closing their mouth. They may look scary as they bare their razor-sharp teeth, but they are actually pumping water to their gills, which is how they breathe.

Eels swim by moving their body in a wave-like motion.

Spotted garden eels live in large colonies near reefs. When feeding, they pop up from their sandy burrows, swaying back and forth like seagrass in the current.

At night, eels come out to hunt. They have weak eyesight, so they use their keen sense of smell to find a tasty meal. When a prey animal swims by, they seize it at lightning speed.

Most eels don't have scales. Instead, they're covered with slippery, slimy mucus, which keeps them from getting scratched when they swim through sharp coral.

Fish, fish, fish

Australian reef fish come in every shape, size, and color. Striped or spotted patterns on a fish help them blend in with the coral. Flat-bodied fish can slip into narrow hiding places in a reef.

The **bluespot butterflyfish** tricks predators with a spot on its tail that looks like an eye. Its hungry enemies can't figure out which way this fish is headed!

The **blue tang** defends itself with a razor-sharp spine at the base of its tail fin that contains a pain-inducing toxin.

A **lionfish** may appear cute and cuddly, but it has a greedy appetite and eats countless young fish on the reef.

When **triggerfish**'s sharp spines stand erect, hungry fish find them tricky to swallow. Triggerfish can also use their spines to lock themselves into a crevice, making it tough for a predator to drag them out.

When threatened, a **blowfish** can puff up into a balloon shape by filling itself with water.

Mandarin fish are some of the most dazzling fish on a reef. They don't have scales for protection; instead, they have slimy, stinky skin that tastes terrible.

Clownfish and sea anemones are best friends. Clownfish become immune to an anemone's sting when they get covered in sticky mucus from its skin, so they can keep safe from predators within an anemone's tentacles. They eat parasites that feed on the anemone, and their bright colors attract animals, which then get zapped and turned into an anemone snack.

**Great Barrier Reef**

The Great Barrier Reef is the largest coral reef system on Earth—so big that it can be seen from space.

The Great Barrier Reef actually includes three thousand different reefs, composed of nearly six hundred species of coral. It encompasses more than nine hundred islands and is home to more than 1,500 kinds of fish.

In many coral species, males and females release their reproductive cells, or spawn, into the ocean at the same time. Corals of the Great Barrier Reef do so every year under a full moon in late spring or early summer, filling the reef with what looks like fairy dust.

Climate change is the greatest threat to the Great Barrier Reef. As the planet gets warmer, so does the ocean temperature. Warmer ocean temperatures lead to coral bleaching.

Bleaching occurs when coral polyps react to the stress of warmer water by expelling the algae that provide them with nutrients. They lose their color and are vulnerable to starvation and disease.

Sadly, the Great Barrier Reef has suffered much damage in recent years. This has impacted the reef's biodiversity, with many sea creatures and plants becoming vulnerable. The reef's future health depends on us—the human race. We must do all we can to save one of the most significant and fragile environments on Earth.

Handfish

Handfish have fins that look like hands. They can swim but prefer to "walk" on their fins to search for food.

Red handfish are found only on shallow rocky reefs in Tasmania. Even though they are bright red, they are tiny and difficult to spot in the seaweed.

The red handfish is one of the world's most critically endangered fish. Only about seventy are believed to be left in the wild.

The biggest threats to the survival of the handfish are pollution, coastal development, and climate change, as well as being collected illegally for aquariums.

Red handfish have a feathery frill above their mouth, which acts like a fishing lure, attracting prey animals.

Unlike many other fish, mother handfish stay with their eggs until they hatch.

 Irukandji

Irukandji are the smallest and one of the most dangerous jellyfish in Australian coastal waters and reefs.

The Irukandji's nearly transparent body and small size make it difficult to spot in the reef waters.

The Irukandji's tentacles resemble a string of pearls. But this is a pearl necklace you don't want to wear!

When stung by an Irukandji, humans experience symptoms that include stomach cramps, nausea, vomiting, headaches, and feelings of impending doom. Sometimes an Irukandji sting can lead to death.

Jellyfish

Jellyfish have been on Earth for millions of years, even before dinosaurs.

Many kinds of jellyfish are found floating through Australian reefs. Many, like the **moon jelly**, pose no danger to humans. But some do, including the Irukandji, which is a species of **box jellyfish**.

Jellyfish are not fish, nor do they taste like jelly. They were named for their wobbly, jelly-ish body.

The **lion's mane jellyfish** is one of the world's largest jellyfish, with gigantic tentacles that can grow more than 100 feet/30 meters long.

Jellyfish don't have many predators. Certain sea turtles prey on them. And some kinds of jellyfish are eaten by humans, often in salads.

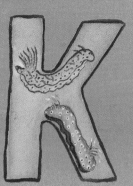

Kunes and kanga nudibranchs

Kunes and kanga nudibranchs are sea slugs found on shallow reefs.

Nudibranchs (pronounced NOO-duh-branks) are sometimes called the jewels of the sea. Their bright colors warn hungry predators that nudibranchs are dangerous! Some are toxic and many taste yucky.

The kanga nudibranch is pale blue with dark-blue lines and yellow dots.

There are hundreds of different kinds of nudibranchs living on Australian reefs, and it is believed there are many more waiting to be discovered.

Like many nudibranchs, the kunes and kanga breathe through flower-like gills on their back.

The kunes nudibranch has a cream and gold body with large purple dots.

The tentacle horns on a nudibranch's head are called rhinophores. They use these to taste and smell and to find their friends. Because the horns stick out, hungry fish try to eat them. Luckily, nudibranchs can hide them in a pocket in their skin.

Leafy sea dragons

Leafy sea dragons look like floating bits of seaweed on the reef.

The leafy sea dragon's frilly appendages allow it to blend in among kelp and other seaweeds. It can also change color, becoming darker in deeper water. Its camouflage protects it from predators and also makes it less visible to the little fish it feeds on.

The leafy sea dragon is found only in Australian waters.

Sea dragons are not dragons but fish related to seahorses.

To move, leafy sea dragons use two thin, nearly invisible fins.

Like seahorses, male sea dragons carry the eggs. When the fry, or babies, are ready to emerge, the male releases them from his special pouch into the water.

To eat, they use their long snout like a drinking straw to suck up their favorite food: miniature shrimp.

Mollusks

Mollusks are soft-bodied sea animals. Reefs are home to thousands of different kinds of mollusks, including clams, oysters, squid, octopuses, cuttlefish, and nudibranchs.

Some types of mollusks, such as **oysters**, **clams**, and **mussels**, have a hard shell for protection. Others, such as **sea slugs**, have no shell, but their bright colors or patterns serve as a warning sign to say they would make a terrible meal.

The **giant triton** is a sea snail and one of the crown-of-thorns sea star's few predators.

The **giant clam** can grow to be about 3 feet/1 meter across and weigh more than 440 pounds/200 kilograms, making it the largest mollusk found on reefs. The shell is so big that a child could curl up inside it!

Giant clams play an essential role for other reef creatures. They offer a place to live for tiny creatures and produce shell material that helps build the reef, and their poop is an important source of food for fish.

Cuttlefish have secret powers! In less than a second, they can change the color, pattern, shape, and texture of their skin in imitation of their surroundings. This is why they're known as the chameleons of the sea.

The giant **cuttlefish** is found only on Australia's reefs and can grow up to a majestic 3 feet/1 meter long!

Ningaloo Reef

Ningaloo Reef is one of the longest fringing coral reefs in the world. It can be reached by a short swim from the beach.

The reef is a popular tourist destination where people can swim with the largest fish in the ocean: the whale shark!

The protective waters of Ningaloo Reef are an ideal breeding area for manta rays and dugongs and a perfect nesting zone for sea turtles.

Dugongs are sea mammals related to manatees. Colonies of up to a thousand dugongs can be found grazing in Ningaloo Marine Park's seagrass beds.

Located off the west coast of Australia, Ningaloo Reef is a feeding ground for many migrating sea animals, including whale sharks, humpback whales, and southern right whales. A nearby gulf is a safe nursery for calves.

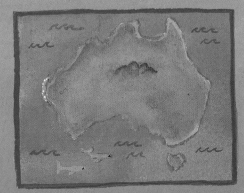

Ningaloo Reef is a protected
World Heritage area. It extends
186 miles/300 kilometers along
the coast and is home to more
than five hundred kinds of fish.

Octopuses

Octopuses are octo-mazing! They have three hearts, eight arms, and blue blood. And what's more, they have one central brain and eight smaller brains, one in each arm, making them very brainy creatures!

Octopuses are the world's greatest contortionists. They are able to squeeze into almost anywhere on a reef—even into a tossed-out bottle or can.

This is a **blanket octopus**. The female is enormous, growing up to 6½ feet/2 meters long. She has a flowing "cape" that makes her appear threatening to predators. Both the cape and the tips of her arms can break off when she is in trouble. The severed arm makes wiggling motions, which confuse a predator while the octopus makes a hasty escape. Sometimes she tears off the poisonous tentacles of a jellyfish and uses them to chase away attackers. For a fast getaway, she can roll her cape under her arms.

The male blanket octopus is smaller than a Ping-Pong ball and weighs forty thousand times less than the female. This is one of the biggest gender size differences in the animal kingdom.

The **blue-ringed octopus** is named after the flashing bright blue circles that appear on its skin when it is threatened. The bite of this tiny octopus can kill a human.

When newly hatched, the deadly blue-ringed octopus is as small as a blueberry.

P Parrotfish

Parrotfish have a beak-shaped mouth and are brightly colored—so it's easy to see how they got their name!

A parrotfish's beaky mouth contains about one thousand teeth, which it uses to graze on algae and crunch coral. Too much algae can smother a reef, so parrotfish have an important job as reef cleaners.

At night, some parrotfish snuggle into a cocoon they make from their own mucus. This is thought to protect them from biting pests while they sleep.

Parrotfish grind up the pieces of coral and poop out the waste as beautiful sand. Many beaches are made of parrotfish poop!

Peacock mantis shrimp

The punch of a peacock mantis shrimp is one of the fastest and strongest in the animal world.

Mantis shrimp have remarkable eyes located on mobile stalks that can rotate in every direction independently.

The peacock mantis shrimp is a type of shrimp known as a smasher. It has powerful club-like limbs that it uses to smash the shells of crabs and mollusks. Its strike speed is lightning fast— fifty times quicker than the blink of an eye. Some mantis shrimp are called spearers; they have sharp spear-like limbs, which they use to stab their prey.

Queensland groupers

Queensland groupers are the largest bony fish found swimming on coral reefs.

This gigantic grouper can grow up to 10 feet/3 meters long and weigh up to half a ton—that's as heavy as an average-sized horse!

Queensland groupers can live for up to fifty years, which is old for a fish.

This huge fish can be found swimming in caves and around shipwrecks on a reef.

It is a slow swimmer and needs to use a surprise attack to catch its dinner. It opens its large mouth, creating strong suction, then swallows up a tasty treat in one enormous gulp.

When a grouper sees a scuba diver, it may become curious and swim over to say hello— it might even pose for a photo!

Crayfish, turtles, and stingrays are among the favorite foods of this jumbo-sized fish.

Rays

Rays are easy to identify by their flat body and wide wings.

Reef-dwelling manta rays are smaller than the giant ocean-dwelling mantas, but they're still impressive, with a whopping wingspan of around 13 feet/ 4 meters. That's about the length of a small car!

Rays sometimes leap out of the water and, for a few seconds, seem to fly like birds.

The oceanic manta ray is the largest ray in the world. These gentle giants have the biggest brain of all fish and are highly intelligent.

A manta ray swims with its mouth open to filter food. When it finds an area to feed, it flips over and over to stay in one place. Alternatively, it can create spinning whirlpools to help steer the food into its mouth.

The spotted pattern on manta rays and eagle rays is unique to each animal, just like human fingerprints.

A mother eagle ray carries her eggs until the babies—called pups—are born and ready to swim away on their own.

An eagle ray has a rounded face with a pointed tip that looks like an eagle's beak. But unlike the bird, this animal has venomous barbs and spines on its tail.

Sea stars

Sea stars are sometimes called starfish, but since they are not a fish, with fins, teeth, scales, and gills, scientists have recently changed their name.

Sea stars come in many different colors and sizes and have differing numbers of arms.

One of the sea star's favorite foods is soft mollusks. A sea star can pry open a mollusk by using its sucker feet to grip and pull it slightly apart. It then feeds by pushing its stomach out through its mouth and into the shell. When it is finished eating, it sucks its stomach back inside.

At the end of each arm, sea stars have simple eyes that can sense light and dark. If a sea star loses an arm, it can grow a new one, including a new eye!

The **crown-of-thorns** is one of the largest sea stars in the world. It is named for the hundreds of sharp poisonous spines on its back and arms.

These aggressive sea stars are known as coral killers. They feed by absorbing all the juices of coral polyps, and each one can destroy more than 100 square feet/ 10 square meters of living coral a year. During population outbreaks, they can eat the coral faster than an area can regenerate.

An outbreak occurs when many crown-of-thorns feed on a reef, destroying large areas. This is one of the leading causes of coral loss on the Great Barrier Reef.

A sea star has hundreds of suckers on its feet, which help it move around. With so many little feet, some sea stars are speedier than you might think. A crown-of-thorns can travel up to 12 miles/ 20 kilometers an hour. That's nearly half as fast as an Olympic sprinter.

Turtles

Six of the world's seven types of sea turtles live in the waters around Australian reefs.

On a reef, sea turtles enjoy a visit to a cleaning station to free their skin and shells from hitchhikers. This spa-like pampering is where small fish remove parasites, dead skin, and heavy barnacles that might weigh a turtle down. In exchange, the cleaner fish enjoy a delicious meal.

Some of the biggest threats to sea turtles are plastic pollution and getting caught in fishing gear. Their survival is also endangered by climate change and coastal development.

A **green turtle**'s diet of seaweed and seagrass gives it a layer of green fat under its shell. These turtles play an important role in maintaining healthy seagrass beds.

Hawksbill turtles feed on marine sponges. When ocean temperatures rise, too many sponges can grow and smother a reef. This turtle eats the sponges, which reduces the population and clears the coral, making room for other sea creatures to flourish.

A **loggerhead** may have thousands of tiny animals and plants, including barnacles and shrimp, living on its shell.

Loggerhead turtles are named for their large heads and strong jaws, which they use to crunch their favorite foods: mollusks, crabs, and urchins.

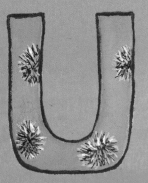

Urchins

Urchins are slow-moving spiky sea creatures that look more like pincushions or flowers than animals.

Sea urchins help the reef by grazing on algae. This allows the corals to thrive. But if a reef is overfished, an outbreak of sea urchins can occur, and this might result in the removal of too much algae, which could hinder reef health.

A sea urchin's hard shell and sharp spines protect it from predators. These creatures may look pretty, but some sea urchin spines are venomous.

The sea urchin has a special mouth with five sharp teeth, called an Aristotle's lantern. It can use these strong teeth to scrape off algae, bite, and even drill a hole into the reef. It can wedge into this carved-out hollow to keep safe from predators and storms.

Violet sea apples

Violet sea apples are sea cucumbers—
the reef's rubbish munchers.

Like all sea cucumbers, the violet sea apple pumps water in and out of its bottom to breathe. Sometimes when a sea cucumber pumps water in, slender pearlfish wiggle inside the sea cucumber and take up residence there.

To escape danger, a violet sea apple can suck in water and puff itself up to the size of a volleyball. After inflating, it floats away on the current.

Violet sea apples scare off predators by vomiting through their mouth and bottom, releasing clouds of poison.

Sea cucumber poop contains several substances that fertilize coral, helping it to grow.

Walking sharks, whitetip reef sharks, wobbegongs, and whale sharks

Whale sharks, whitetip reef sharks, walking sharks, and wobbegongs spend time on Australian reefs. Luckily, these four sharks are mostly harmless to humans.

Whitetip reef sharks sometimes stack on top of each other under coral banks and in caves to rest during the day. Unlike some sharks, whitetips do not need to move to breathe. At night, these sharks are skillful solo hunters.

The straggly, whiskered fringe around a **wobbegong**'s head makes it look a bit like a shaggy rug—and adds to its camouflage on the reef.

Other sharks observed on Australian reefs include great white sharks, black-tip reef sharks, leopard sharks, tawny nurse sharks, lemon sharks, tiger sharks, and hammerheads.

At low tide, the **walking shark** can "walk" on the reef, outside of the water. It uses its fins like feet, on a search for sea creatures trapped in exposed tidal pools.

The **whale shark** is the biggest of all reef fish. It can grow up to a humongous 39 feet/ 12 meters long. Its favorite meal is plankton—tiny creatures that it sucks into its wide mouth like a vacuum cleaner.

Whale sharks have hundreds of tiny teeth on their eyeballs, which are thought to be used for protection from predators since they don't have eyelids.

Xanthid crabs

Xanthid crabs are a family of crabs that live on Australian reefs and are recognizable by their black-tipped claws.

Xanthid crabs are brightly colored—but beware! Some are highly poisonous to humans, even in a very small amount.

One kind of xanthid crab, the **furry coral crab**, helps keep the reef healthy by slowing down a damaging disease called white syndrome. These crabs eat the tissue and tiny microscopic creatures located at the source of the disease.

Like most crabs, xanthid crabs can use their claws as nifty tools for fighting, as scissors for cutting, and as chopsticks for eating.

Yellowtail barracudas

The yellowtail barracuda is one of the smallest barracudas seen cruising on coral reefs.

Yellowtail barracudas swim in schools during the day and hunt alone at night, sneaking through reefs searching for food.

These sleek fish have a pointy head, powerful jaws, and razor-sharp teeth. Their forked tail fin helps them swim with super-fast bursts of speed.

There are many different types of barracudas in Australian reef waters. The largest one is the great barracuda. It is a ferocious, sly hunter that uses agility and speed to catch its prey. Its nickname is the "tiger of the sea."

Barracudas use their keen eyesight to search for anything moving or shiny in the water to eat.

Bright-red **coral guard crabs** help keep reefs free from troublemakers by using their sharp pincers to bite the feet and spines of the pesky crown-of-thorns sea star.

Zebra seahorses

Zebra seahorses are found only on reefs in Australia and are named for their long zebra-shaped face and their black and white stripes.

Seahorses use their flexible tail to grab onto coral and plants, similar to how some monkeys can hang upside down in a tree by their tail. During a storm, seahorses use their tail as an anchor to keep from floating away.

Most seahorses pair up with a partner for life. Sometimes they join their tails and swim together, similar to humans holding hands as they walk.